YOUR KNOWLEDGE HAS VALUE

- We will publish your bachelor's and
  master's thesis, essays and papers

- Your own eBook and book -
  sold worldwide in all relevant shops

- Earn money with each sale

Upload your text at www.GRIN.com
and publish for free

Nassef M. Adiong

The Probabilty of Humanitarian Intervention as Framework for Human Security

GRIN Verlag

Bibliografische Information der Deutschen Nationalbibliothek:

Die Deutsche Bibliothek verzeichnet diese Publikation in der Deutschen National-
bibliografie; detaillierte bibliografische Daten sind im Internet über http://dnb.d-
nb.de/ abrufbar.

Dieses Werk sowie alle darin enthaltenen einzelnen Beiträge und Abbildungen
sind urheberrechtlich geschützt. Jede Verwertung, die nicht ausdrücklich vom
Urheberrechtsschutz zugelassen ist, bedarf der vorherigen Zustimmung des Verla-
ges. Das gilt insbesondere für Vervielfältigungen, Bearbeitungen, Übersetzungen,
Mikroverfilmungen, Auswertungen durch Datenbanken und für die Einspeicherung
und Verarbeitung in elektronische Systeme. Alle Rechte, auch die des auszugsweisen
Nachdrucks, der fotomechanischen Wiedergabe (einschließlich Mikrokopie) sowie
der Auswertung durch Datenbanken oder ähnliche Einrichtungen, vorbehalten.

Imprint:

Copyright © 2011 GRIN Verlag GmbH
Druck und Bindung: Books on Demand GmbH, Norderstedt Germany
ISBN: 978-3-656-01682-3

This book at GRIN:

http://www.grin.com/en/e-book/179152/the-probabilty-of-humanitarian-interven-
tion-as-framework-for-human-security

GRIN - Your knowledge has value

Der GRIN Verlag publiziert seit 1998 wissenschaftliche Arbeiten von Studenten, Hochschullehrern und anderen Akademikern als eBook und gedrucktes Buch. Die Verlagswebsite www.grin.com ist die ideale Plattform zur Veröffentlichung von Hausarbeiten, Abschlussarbeiten, wissenschaftlichen Aufsätzen, Dissertationen und Fachbüchern.

Visit us on the internet:

http://www.grin.com/

http://www.facebook.com/grincom

http://www.twitter.com/grin_com

THE PROBABILITY OF HUMANITARIAN INTERVENTION
AS FRAMEWORK FOR HUMAN SECURITY

Nassef M. Adiong[1]

Abstract

The paper aims to present a probable humanitarian intervention as framework of human security. It objectifies humanitarian intervention as an element that will make human security autonomous but not separate nor fully independent from non-traditional security. Several literatures confuses the two terms as synonymous with each other, where others differentiated them explicitly. Thus the essay will address the ambiguity of both conceptions and discuss humanitarian intervention not as a different concept from human security but argues that it may be part and parcel of it, and in fact a possible framework to explain the paradigm of human security autonomous to non-traditional security. This contribution aspires for a sound, simple yet clear and unambiguous interpretation of human security to the evolving field of security especially as a sub-discipline of International Relations. In addition, it will also contend that there is a considerable middle way for both human security and non-traditional security in meeting a tangency point, and that is, a re-conceptualized version of human rights.

Keywords

Humanitarian Intervention, Human Security, Non-Traditional Security, Humanitarian Development, Human Rights

Purpose and Objective

Why there's a need to separate human security from non-traditional security? In this line of inquiry, we need to consider the aim of this paper as mentioned above, thus question should also fit to the construction of essay. The proponent wants to emphasize that he is not separating human security from non-traditional security because in his second hypothesis he is also interested in looking for a middle way for both conceived ideas. This is not to separate them but to make the conception of human security autonomous from the conception of non-traditional security. Related literatures have confused both conceptions and increased its ambiguity which directed some scholars and practitioners to formulate their own interpretations of human security and non-traditional security. The proponent is confused when he read studies stating both conceptions identical in nature and hence, equal footing status, when in fact it exacerbated further confusions and tensions.

Consequently, the primal objective of this study is to remove the confusion that these two terms are facing. To exclude their identical character we need explanatory power to claim and defend our main idea, and what the author is thinking is to present human security with its own explanatory power to make a (standing) paradigm coherent and clear. Further, the purpose is not a matter of challenging what the other scholars have said but to add another view or element to the diverse interpretations of human security vis-à-vis non-traditional security. And his objective is to simply interpret human security as clear as possible and without attached ambiguousness. The proponent's essay will first look into the evolution and development of the conception of the term 'security' then will discuss the ambiguity between the two conceptions and provide humanitarian intervention as the explanatory framework to establish its autonomy.

---

[1] He is a PhD student in International Relations at the Middle East Technical University.

The Etymology of 'Security'

In its broadest and academic term, "security" has been defined contemporarily as being that special type of politics in which specified developments are socially constructed threats, having an existential quality to cover values and/or assets of human collectivities and leading to a call for emergency measures.[2] However, surveying the old traditional perceptions of security dating back from Plato, Aristotle, Confucius, to Rousseau, Kant, Kautilya, to Hobbes, Machiavelli and to Morgenthau, the proponent found a linkage of security study in providing answers to human physiological needs that is interpreted in varied disciplines of Philosophy, Political Science and International Relations. To Plato such path leading to security was presented in his ideal republic. The total security, both spiritual and material, was brought about the creation of a new society and all its institutions based on the right principles of social existence. Plato related these principles to the idea of the universal Good as governing nature.[3]

For Aristotle the quest for security was connected with his idea of fullness of being and ideal nature.[4] This took the form of instinctive striving after perfection as embodied in the species. In the area of man's social or political life, security arrangements manifested themselves in certain types of social systems said to be in harmony with nature or in conformity with man's striving after full development of himself or the Good's life. For Confucius security was associated with commitments to certain universal principles of conduct. The ultimate aim was to bring about a condition of universal social harmony and stability. Goodness of human nature was often assumed which, if damaged, could be restored mainly by proper education.[5]

For Rousseau, the quest for security diverts from the man's attempt to return to his natural condition, which Rousseau portrayed as the natural goodness of man, and man's quest for political legitimacy.[6] To Kant, security is the recognition of the rational possibility of a universal peace. However, for the Indian thinker Kautilya contends the holding of an opinion that universal egoism is made permanent security impossible.[7] He developed a system of security where this was treated as diverse strategies by which, given the egoist nature of man, social living or security, could be made manageable, and so, relative security might be attained. Cicero, an Italian philosopher, is the first who is closer to identifying security as human security whereby he described it as the absence of anxiety upon which the fulfilled life depends.[8]

Hobbes' argument of an organized society where security prevails takes place lies in the shadow of the Leviathan-ruler, ever prepared to use his sword to enforce the conditions of the social contract, which is the original choice of anarchic men.[9] Buzan and Wæver opined that Hobbes' premise was too individualistic (not organicist or romantic like the German ancestors of realism).[10] His starting point is an individual who has a right to self defense, but that individual pursuit of self-preservation is vulnerable. The basic Hobbesian argument that a social contract constructing a commonwealth was necessary or at least preferable for security, and thereby liberty, for they found it necessary to tame and

---

[2] Barry Buzan and Ole Wæver. *Liberalism and Security: The Contradictions of the Liberal Leviathan,* Copenhagen Peace Research Institute, April 1998 [database on-line]; available at www.ciaonet.org/wps/bub02/index.html, in November 22, 2009.

[3] Estrella D. Solidum, Teresita D. Saldivar-Sali and Roman Dubsky. "Security in a New Perspective," in Estrella D. Solidum, *The Sall State: Security and World Peace,* (Manila: Kalikasan Press, 1991), p. 13.

[4] Ibid. p. 14.

[5] Ibid. p. 15.

[6] Ibid. p. 15.

[7] Ibid. p. 16.

[8] P.H. Liotta and Taylor Owen, "Why Human Security," *The Whitehead Journal of Diplomacy and International Relations,* Seton Hall University, Winter/Spring 2006, pp. 37-54.

[9] Solidum, Saldivar-Sali and Dubsky, "Security in a New Perspective," p. 16.

[10] Buzan and Wæver, "Liberalism and Security," [database on-line]; available at www.ciaonet.org/wps/bub02/index.html, in November 22, 2009.

constrain the state. On the other hand, Machiavelli argued that the possibility of relative security may exist only if a society or a statesman behave as a disciplined and responsible citizen, or alternatively, if a regime is run in an authoritarian manner with force being used generously to repress anarchic tendencies in man.[11]

In my understanding, security occurs due to the fact that man is responsible of protecting himself from the threats that he thinks exist with a purpose of building a securitized environment, and for him to live by sufficing and enjoying his satisfaction(s). The means and ways on how to build a securitized environment should also be considered. Like for example, are we talking of foreign aids or an effective government?

Theorizing Security in International Relations

In this prism, the proponent will going to discuss the differing security theories from the perspective of International Relations and how time impacted its evolution of being conceptualized. Theoretical interest in security from the perspective of realism acquired importance in the 16th and 17th centuries with mercantilist ideas of national protectionism. While an important phase in recent thought on security has been the era of the "Cold War," where the search for national and world-wide security has tended to crystallize itself in terms of two competing camps, one associated with the Soviet Union and the other with the United States. In contemporary, one view of security is defined as the protection of values previously acquired or as high value expectancy in the sense of continued unmolested enjoyment of one's possessions.[12] Here, security, when viewed as a topic of international politics, is generally perceived as the ability of the state to protect its way of life, its "core values," meaning its territorial integrity and political independence.

Within the context of the power paradigm, security conceived as the absence of threats to national status or values which is attained or maintained only through the accumulation of instrument of power. Morgenthau sees the issue of security within the context of international politics where sovereign state pursues its own peculiar national interest.[13] Obviously, during the Cold War there has been a tendency to emphasize balance of power and military power which are thoughts of as useful for protecting national security or interest. On the other hand, since the onset of Cold War, liberal theory has downplayed security and security studies mostly ignored or dismissed liberalism.[14] Liberalism challenged the logic of security by asserting that the supposedly permanent realist world of fear can in fact be not only alleviated, but possibly even replaced altogether. If states act according to a liberal logic of maximizing absolute gains and generally prioritize economics over politics, then the war problematic to security will become marginal, and both security studies and the security institutions of the state will eventually become redundant.[15]

Redefining Security: The Post-Cold War Impact

Security has been traditionally interpreted as a mechanism of protecting the national interest of states through foreign policy making and implementation. It has long been considered as a priori of legitimizing the territorial integrity of the wholeness of state and used to frame states in declaring war against others in times of conflict and hostility. Security also measures the capabilities of state with regard to physical or material capacities in securing itself by enhancing defense strategy, military power, steel industry, war armaments and intelligence operations.

---

[11] Solidum, Saldivar-Sali and Dubsky, "Security in a New Perspective," p. 17.

[12] Ibid. p. 18.

[13] Ibid. p. 19.

[14] Buzan and Wæver, "Liberalism and Security," [database on-line]; available at www.ciaonet.org/wps/bub02/index.html, in November 22, 2009.

[15] Ibid. [database on-line]; available at www.ciaonet.org/wps/bub02/index.html, in November 22, 2009.

During the World War I, the British have been busy desecuritizing issues in the sense of social democracy while in World War II up to the Cold War; Americans had introduced a new paradigm which is securitizing issues through their liberal perspective. Here security was shaped by the contradictory pressures of reacting to Soviet Communism as a broad-spectrum external threat, and containing the risk of domestic military threats to the liberty of American civil society. Therefore securitization is not just a call for political priority, but if need be, for permission to break the normal rules of politics, i.e., by using force, by taking executive powers, or by imposing secrecy.[16] It is when the move that takes politics beyond the established rules of the game and frames the issue either as a special kind of politics or as above politics and may refers to the classification of and consensus about certain phenomena, persons or entities as existential threats requiring emergency measures.[17]

Securitization is thus mostly about calls for closure against things perceived as existentially threatening and further, the consensual establishment of threat needs to be sufficient so as to produce substantial political effects. What constitutes an existential threat is thus viewed by Copenhagen School stating that it depends on a shared understanding of what is meant by such a danger to security. Threat may be classified into three: (1) Actual threats are existing conditions that can, at any moment, reduce security; (2) potential threats are conditions tending to reduce security but are not transformable to actual threats due to some constraints; and (3) fictitious threats are conditions that are perceived to reduce security but do not really exist.[18]

In this era different threats were conceived ranging from who will be the next enemy of the single sole superpower in the world, i.e., of course the US. Epidemic diseases like SARS, HIV Aids virus, Swine Flu virus among others that were spreading faster to poor continents (Africa, Asia, and South America), environmental challenges which includes the infamous climate change (global warming to be specific), causes that aggravate the worst situations for refugees, displaced persons (internally or externally) and particularly of the stateless population like in the Palestinian case, the transnational character of terrorism, global financial crisis and other conditions regionally or globally that makes the lives of human beings vulnerable to these new perceived, actual or existential threats. These are the new enemies of state.

This paved the way of the birth of non-traditional security wherein the people not the state as the referent object which should be protected and securitized. It is the security of an individual for adequate and stable conditions that addresses developmental issues. It is also considered as a shift from the bipolar threat of the Cold War to the threats considered as vulnerabilities in human conditions. However, human security can also be define broadly similar to non-traditional security in toto with its ontological propositions (the existence of their being) and epistemological presuppositions (the acquisition of knowledge per se), but how can we put human security not identical to non-traditional security? What explanatory framework can we used to defend the predicate of the aforementioned statement, i.e., human security's autonomous nature from non-traditional security? These questions are central to the proposed purpose and objective of the study, which will be discuss in the succeeding sections.

Human Security or Non-Traditional Security?

Non-traditional security was put entrenched side-by-side human security in the post-Cold War period. There were two directions where human security was conceptualized and developed: (1) the approach taken by the Canadian government, which in her own words was "adopted and established a network of like-minded states who subscribed to the concept," i.e., responsibility to protect, and was

---

[16] Ibid. [database on-line]; available at www.ciaonet.org/wps/bub02/index.html, in November 22, 2009.

[17] Mely Caballero-Anthony and Ralf Emmers, "The Dynamics of Securitization in Asia," in Ralf Emmers, Mely Caballero-Anthony and Amitav Acharya, *Studying Non-Traditional Security in Asia: Trends and Issue*, (Singapore: Marshall Cavendish Academic, 2006), p. 23.

[18] Solidum, Saldivar-Sali and Dubsky, "Security in a New Perspective," p. 28.

published in the 2005 Human Security Report. (2) The UNDP approach which was also reflected in the work of the United Nations High-Level Panel on Threats, Challenges and Change.[19] This approach according to Kaldor emphasized the interrelatedness of different types of security and the importance of development as a security strategy.

A misleading interpretation to human security is the so-called 'population security' popularized by former US Secretary of State Condoleezza Rice, she meant for giving the population the basic needs they want by securing their environments against perpetrators who increases their insecurity. This conception is not intact and clear because it permeates that you must defeat first those perpetrators who you perceived as enemies without mentioning who are them and how can you defeat them, is it by force or by any other means? Another attempt that adds to the confusion and vagueness vis-à-vis human security and non-traditional security is the term, "transborder security," which concerns with threats that are non-military ones that threatens the political and social integrity of a state or the health and quality of life of its inhabitants.

Historically, in 1994 the United Nations Commission on Human Security defined human security as the protection of "the vital core of all human lives in ways that enhance human freedom and fulfillment."[20] In 1998, the Canadian concept paper defined human security as "freedom from pervasive threats to people's rights, their safety, or even their lives."[21] However, for Kaldor it is a combination of these two interpretations, she defined it in three aspects: (1) It is about the security of individuals and the communities in which they live rather than the security of the state. (2) It is about the interrelated nature of security, the link between 'freedom from fear' and 'freedom from want'. (3) It is about the global nature of security and the blurring of the distinction between internal security, which is supposed to be guaranteed through a rule of law, and external security, which is guaranteed through defense policies.[22]

Moreover, it incorporates terms like crisis management and stability but goes beyond it because the term also encompasses a notion of justice and sustainability. Kaldor's version of human security is somehow problematic because it involves everything from crisis management, interventionist characteristic against sovereignist, justice, human rights, human development, and etc. The element of time and space is nowhere to be found. The explanatory framework is weak, confusing and unclear. Her human security paradigm can also be considered as the non-traditional security paradigm by emphasizing the interrelatedness of different types of security.

If comprising all types of security in one paradigm how can she be able to defend the modification of referent object(s) as time and space changes? If humans or human activities are the perpetrators of perceived existential threats on aggravating global warming then the environment or the Mother Nature (specifically the biodiversity of an ecological community) is the referent object that must be protected and securitized. How can she also explain extinct or endanger animals caused by human negligence and harmful activities? Thus the interrelatedness or encompassing all fora of describing and defining human security is problematic.

---

[19] Mary Kaldor, *Human Security: Reflections on Globalization and Intervention*, Cambridge, U.K., Polity Press, 2007, pp. 182-187.

[20] P.H. Liotta and Taylor Owen, "Why Human Security," p. 37.

[21] Marlies Glasius, "Human Security from Paradigm Shift to Operationalization: Job Description for a Human Security Worker," *Security Dialogue* 39, 2008, p. 33.

[22] Mary Kaldor, *We have to Think about the Security of Individuals rather than the Protection of Borders*, Boston Review, Febraury/March Archive of 2005 [Database on-line]; available at www.bostonreview.net/BR30.1/kaldor.php, in November 25, 2009.

Figure 1. A Putative Description of the Research Problem

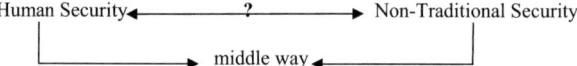

The double pointed straight line arrows between human security and non-traditional security represents the ambiguity of the two terms for it reflects notions in their identical character of conceptualizations, thus a question mark is at the middle of the straight line. The purpose of this paper is to break the straight lines into broken lines which it will possibly represent the shifting away of human security as an autonomous term and not identical to non-traditional security. It doesn't mean that if they are not identical, similarities will be totally disregarded.

It is still strongly to emphasize the nature of their similarities with regards to the primacy of human rights as the bond between them. The change of the actor level is very important since it developed a new subject-matter in the security field consonance with the contemporary world. The 'middle way' or a link that even the line is broken there still left for understanding both terms of sameness by incorporating a reconceptualized human rights version. The middle way serves as a link that human security is still a component of non-traditional security, even though the paper is trying to make human security autonomous from non-traditional security.

In line with the inquiries posited above, I suggests of using the arithmetic method of adding and subtracting elements which regarded essential in clarifying a simple yet clear conceptualization of human security. Thus humanitarian intervention will be the only added element in reconceptualizing human security and individuals will be its referent object in times where political chaos and hostility causes insecurity to increase.

The Humanitarian Intervention Framework

The expression of humanitarian sentiments in world politics is a product of changing historical and social processes. World or domestic events alter or affect different sentiments that individuals experiences. It is left for the international community in addressing graved humanitarian crisis like what had happened in Rwanda (1994) and Sbrenica (1995). Presently, Sudan's Darfur is also facing this kind of tragic and worst problem could ever happen in a state or community of peoples.

Traditionally, intervention has been defined as a forcible breach of sovereignty that interferes in state's internal affairs. The legality of forcible humanitarian intervention is a matter of dispute between restrictionists and counter-restrictionists.[23] The restrictionists perspective pointed out that: (1) States will not intervene for primarily humanitarian reasons. (2) States are not allowed to risk their soldiers' lives on humanitarian crusades. (3) States will abuse a right of humanitarian intervention using it as a cloak to promote national interests. (4) States will apply principles of humanitarian intervention selectively. (5) Disagreement on what principles should govern a right of humanitarian intervention. For the counter-restrictionists perspective raises significant questions like: (1) Protection of human rights. (2) A customary right of humanitarian intervention. (3) The moral choice of states to involve in humanitarian intervention. These questions were very controversial among lawyers of international law and raise the ire of the authority of the international judicial bodies, e.g., International Criminal Court (ICC).[24]

---

[23] Nicholas J. Wheeler and Alex J. Bellamy (2nd ed.), "Humanitarian Intervention and World Politics" in John Baylis and Steve Smith, *The Globalization of World Politics: An Introduction to International Relations*, (Oxford, U.K.: Oxford University Press, 2001), p. 470.
[24] Ibid. pp. 470-493.

Remember when the Pre-Trial Chamber I of the International Criminal Court (ICC) issued a warrant for the arrest of Omar Hassan Ahmad Al Bashir, President of Sudan, last March 4, 2009 for war crimes and crimes against humanity. He is suspected of being criminally responsible, as an indirect co-perpetrator, for intentionally directing attacks against an important part of the civilian population of Darfur such as murdering, exterminating, raping, torturing and forcibly transferring large numbers of civilians, and pillaging their property. This is the first warrant of arrest ever issued for a sitting Head of State by the ICC.[25]

Presenting the case of explaining different interpretations of humanitarian intervention proves it can be an explanatory framework in dealing with the notion of creating an autonomous human security as a simple and clear paradigm. Some of the arguments borrowed from Kaldor's principles of human security are considered essential but with slight difference of interpretation by dividing it unto ontology which precedes epistemology.

The ontological assumptions were the primacy of human rights (making human lives as point of reference of the new subject matter or an actor level), creation of legitimate political authority (these are institutions which have the mandate of the people of protecting them through their means and ends) and belief on effective multilateralism (it is a matter of making agreements or binding treatise with other states, non-state actors and probably community of people in taking actions to address political hostility and chaos). The epistemological presuppositions were the bottom-up approach (developmental tools like dialogue, communication and diplomacy are imperative to capture criminals that committed grave slanders and crimes against humanity), integrated regional approach (focus on addressing the spillover characteristic of political chaos, conflict and hostility) and clear and transparent strategic direction by states or member of the international community that carried out humanitarian intervention.[26]

These know-how approaches of philosophical methodology is paramount on understanding humanitarian intervention as an important element that makes human security differs from the broadness conception of non-traditional security. An excellent modification of humanitarian intervention since the post-Cold War is the 1998 Canadian version making it as 'responsibility to protect' or R2P from slanderous actions perpetuated by militias hired by the government in hiding their cloak of interests. The principle of 'responsibility to protect' aims to prevent escalating casualties, react on the other perpetrators including the government, rebuild the nation from its ruins through aids, and reviving a healthy political environment.

Taking the case of Rwanda in operationalizing humanitarian intervention (R2P version) of human security, we can see that three stages or pedestal were asserted in bringing back to the normal status quo of the Tutsis and Hutus. My three pedestal of achieving a state of normalcy after a horrendous catastrophe were: (1) short-term security as the first stage or the peace-making stage, (2) medium-term security as the second stage or the peace-building security, and (3) long-term security as the last stage of attaining normalcy or the peace-keeping stage.

The former rebel group became the police in Rwanda due to saving the lives of Tutsis and moderate Hutus from prosecutions. Their short-term security is to provide first basic physiological needs such as food, clothing and shelter to the surviving victims of genocide. The medium-term security is the accession to new integrated and comparative educational policies by building common values and knowledge among the two ethnic groups. The long-term security is represented by creating political amalgamation and acculturation process between the victims and the framed/conservative Hutus.

---

[25] International Criminal Court, Pre-Trial Chamber 1, *Situation in Darfur, Sudan: In the Case of the Prosecutor v. Omar Hassan Ahmad Al Bashir (Warrant of Arrest)* [database on-line]; available at www.icc-cpi.int/iccdocs/doc/doc639078.pdf, in November 27, 2009.

[26] Mary Kaldor, "Human Security," pp. 185-192.

Table. Differences on the Three Major Types of Security

Type of Security	Referent Object	Responsibility to Protect	Possible Threats
Traditional Security	The State	The Integrity of the State	Interstate War, Nuclear Proliferation, Revolution
Non-Traditional Security	Living and Non-living things	The Integrity of both Living and Non-living things	Encompassing all vulnerable economic, social, environmental, and political conditions
Human Security	Individual	The Integrity of an Individual	Genocide, Ethnic Cleansing, Crimes against Humanity

A Reconceptualized 'Human Rights'

R.J. Vincent idea on "human rights" is actually synonymous with his reconceptualized human rights, where he termed it as "basic rights."[27] Historically, human rights were justified and defined in an abstract way of reasoning, that are, the first one is equated to natural or canon law for human beings have the same rights because all of them are members of human community, thus it is universal. The second one is the establishment of formal obligations, treatise among societies or authorities and mutual obligations and rights are defined by acceptance of both parties. The third one which is different from the two aforementioned abstract reasons is the notion of cultural relativism that involves a non-universal doctrine because it is cultural specific in view of different civilizations.[28]

He defined basic right to life as rights that are necessary for the enjoyment of other rights. He considered right to security, subsistence and freedom as requirements for benevolent survival.[29] On the other hand, he laid three arguments concerning the solidarist debate in English School of International Relations: (1) humanitarian intervention means if the state violate the basic right to life and having a minimum content on containing rights to security and subsistence, (2) legitimacy is when a state's legitimacy is recognized by other states, and (3) involves unity and diversity in international society and which content of basic rights must be kept confidential, again the idea of *pacta sunt servanda*.[30]

The arguments presented above reflects on how the notion of human rights be reconceptualized to fit its status as a *via media* to human security and non-international security. It is in this regard that incorporating a convergence of both 'freedom from fear' and 'freedom from want' are imperative and salient elements that would determine a new version of human rights. These two factors reflects the universal notion of human rights; stating freedom from pervasive threats to access basic needs, and protect their lives and achieve fulfillment. This links human security and non-traditional security since both highlight the primacy of human rights as the linking variable to both paradigms.

---

[27] R. J. Vincent, *Human Rights and international Relations*, (U.K.: Cambridge University Press, 1986), p. 4.

[28] Ibid. pp. 4-19.

[29] Ibid. p. 17.

[30] R. J. Vincent, *Nonintervention and International Order*, (Princeton, New Jersey: Princeton University Press, 1974), pp. 327-389.

Conclusion

Since the proponent has described his idea on how to establish human security autonomous from non-traditional security by instituting humanitarian intervention as a probable explanatory framework, the proponent contemplates on the possibility of stating its concluding remarks of the essay. Below is the matrix that clearly outlines and detail the difference between the two securities.

Figure 2. The Answer to Figure 1.

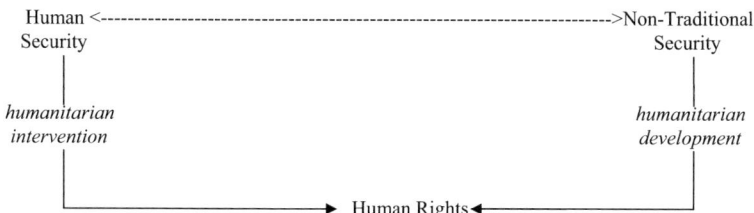

The premise is to differentiate both conceptions which will need two differing explanatory frameworks. Since his contribution resonates on the humanitarian intervention of human security, he surmised non-traditional security as broad and general conception that mainly addresses issues on human development concomitant interrelatedness of different types of security. He, then, relegated its framework as humanitarian development. The framework the proponent forcibly put to non-traditional security needs lots of work for future researcher who would also dwell on the same endeavor he undertook with human security.

The debate on humanitarian intervention between restrictionists and counter-restrictionists regarding (1) who shapes, dictates, interpret human rights, (2) what constitute a moral right of an individual, (3) were there limitations of ethical responsibilities of agents (with international status) in global politics -- are the research inquiries or questions needed to be elaborate and ponder upon. For example, is the arrest order issued by the International Criminal Court to the head of state of Sudan, an exception to the immunity bestowed to heads of states when they agreed on the Vienna Convention of Diplomatic Relations in 1964?

There are several ideas conceived by man that later appeared conflicting or contradicting with his former constructed ideas. There will be debates and challenges whether the implementation of humanitarian intervention is right or wrong, or whether human rights constitute a definition based on different cultures and societies or union of cosmopolitan understanding. However, it will not change the fact that both parties must arrived at a compromise decision and act based on common understanding to address the phenomena, complex or not.

Consequently, assessing the arguments, the proponent therefore concludes that human security may become autonomous from non-traditional security by relegating humanitarian intervention as a probable determining explanatory framework, and that a reconceptualized notion of 'human rights' may be considered the possible middle way. In the fifth section (subheading) of this essay, the discussion of some differing interpretations which scholars undertook made both conceptions confusing whether they are similar or identical. It is in this regard that the essay suggested solution to the confusions entailed within conceptions of different labels/names. The proponent presented the discussions on human security and non-traditional security frameworks, wherein he concentrated on the framework of human security.

The complexity of humanitarian intervention made it possible to become a (standing) framework for human security to build its autonomy by simplifying the conception as clear, simple and unambiguous to comprehend. On the other hand, the task of exploring the framework of non-traditional security will be given to future researchers and scholars interested on the same research. The middle way represents their sameness with regard to the primacy of human rights as the only element that links or bonds them altogether. It does not mean that the highlighted human rights are identical with each other in all aspects of conception.

Recommendation

First, the proponent recommends to future interested researchers who will explore the same research agendum by embarking an extensive research delineating 'human security' from 'non-traditional security' through determining the factors, elements or variables imperative in showing such delineation or quasi-differences so as to further emphasize the purpose of making it simple, clear and stating an unambiguous interpretation or conception. Secondly, present varied or several case studies that will fully support the operationalization of redefined humanitarian intervention. Though in this matter the proponent failed to extensively discuss and explore. Finally, a case on non-traditional security which regarded humanitarian development as an explanatory framework may also be a feasible and plausible task.

Bibliography

Buzan, Barry and Ole Wæver. *Liberalism and Security: The Contradictions of the Liberal Leviathan,* Copenhagen Peace Research Institute, April 1998 [database on-line]; available at www.ciaonet.org/wps/bub02/index.html, in November 22, 2009.
Caballero-Anthony, Mely and Ralf Emmers, "The Dynamics of Securitization in Asia," in Ralf Emmers, Mely Caballero-Anthony and Amitav Acharya, *Studying Non-Traditional Security in Asia: Trends and Issue,* (Singapore: Marshall Cavendish Academic, 2006).
Glasius, Marlies, "Human Security from Paradigm Shift to Operationalization: Job Description for a Human Security Worker," *Security Dialogue* 39, 2008.
International Criminal Court, Pre-Trial Chamber 1, *Situation in Darfur, Sudan: In the Case of the Prosecutor v. Omar Hassan Ahmad Al Bashir (Warrant of Arrest)* [database on-line]; available at www.icc-cpi.int/iccdocs/doc/doc639078.pdf, in November 27, 2009.
Kaldor, Mary, *Human Security: Reflections on Globalization and Intervention,* Cambridge, U.K., Polity Press, 2007.
Kaldor , Mary, *We have to Think about the Security of Individuals rather than the Protection of Borders,* Boston Review, Febraury/March Archive of 2005 [Database on-line]; available at www.bostonreview.net/BR30.1/kaldor.php, in November 25, 2009.
Liotta, P.H. and Taylor Owen, "Why Human Security," *The Whitehead Journal of Diplomacy and International Relations,* Seton Hall University, Winter/Spring 2006.
Solidum, Estrella D., Teresita D. Saldivar-Sali and Roman Dubsky. "Security in a New Perspective," in Estrella D. Solidum, *The Sall State: Security and World Peace,* (Manila: Kalikasan Press, 1991).
Vincent, R. J., *Human Rights and international Relations,* (U.K.: Cambridge University Press, 1986).
----------*Nonintervention and International Order,* (Princeton, New Jersey: Princeton University Press, 1974).
Wheeler, Nicholas J. and Alex J. Bellamy (2nd ed.), "Humanitarian Intervention and World Politics" in John Baylis and Steve Smith, *The Globalization of World Politics: An Introduction to International Relations,* (Oxford, U.K.: Oxford University Press, 2001).